This book is dedicated to the memory of our mothers

Lillian McKenzie and Alice Jane Coughlin

With Love and Appreciation!

About the author and the illustrator

Cousins, Maribeth and Joanne brought their love for sign language and illustration together to create this book. It is the first book of their Signing with MariJo Series. We hope you like it!

Maribeth McKenzie MacDonald www.signingwithmaribeth.com
Joanne Coughlin www.onceuponapaintedwall.com

Benefits of Baby Sign Language

- Baby Signing experts believe that frustration and tantrums can be avoided by closing the gap between the desire to communicate and the ability to do so.

- Infants from about six months of age can begin to learn basic signs, which cover such objects and concepts as "thirsty", "milk", "water", "hungry", "sleepy", "pacifier", and "more".

- On average, babies who are exposed to sign language verbalize earlier than babies only exposed to spoken language.

- ASL is the 3rd most commonly used language in the USA.

- And - It's Fun!

Hello

Hello: Put your hand to your forehead, four fingers extended, cross your thumb in front of your palm. Extend your hand outward and away from your body. (don't forget to smile)

Mother

Mother: Touch the tip of your chin with your thumb, fingers are outstretched.
*Female signs are signed at the chin.

Father

Father: Touch the middle of your forehead with your thumb, fingers are outstretched. *Male signs are signed at the head.

Grandmother

Grandmother: Start with sign for "Mother" and move your hand forward twice. Mother's mother.

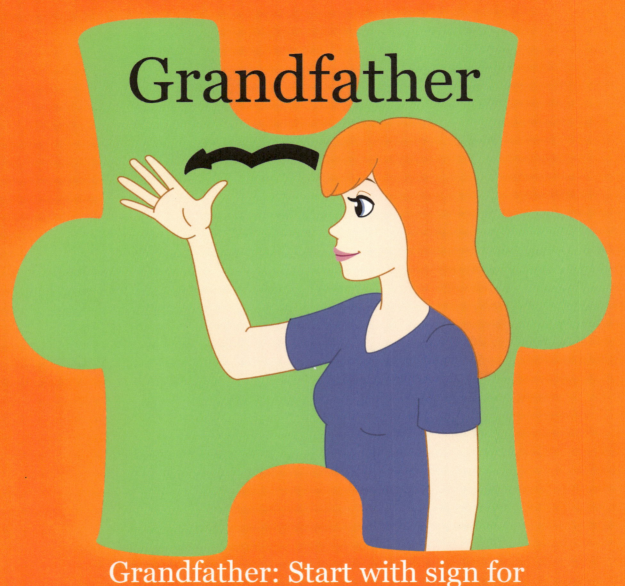

Grandfather

Grandfather: Start with sign for "Father" and move your hand forward twice. Father's father.

Brother

Brother: Sign "Boy". Make both hands into an "L" shape with your index finger and thumb extended. Bring your right hand down to your chest touching the left hand.

Sister: Sign "Girl". Make both hands into an "L" shape with your index finger and thumb extended. Start with your thumb on your jawline and bring your hand down to your chest touching the left hand.

Please: Place your flat hand over the center of your chest. Move your hand in a clockwise motion a few times.

No: Take your index finger together with your middle finger and tap them with your thumb. Shake your head no.

Yes: Make a fist and bob it up and down. Looks like a head nodding yes.

Thank You

Thank you: Place your hands near your lips, fingers together. Move your hand forward and a bit down in the direction of the person you are thanking. (don't forget to smile)

Hungry

Hungry: Make your hand into a c-shape with your palm facing your body. Start with your hand around your neck and move it down. Like food going down into your stomach.

Eat: Also the sign for food. Fingers together, motion putting food in the mouth.

Drink

Drink: Make your hand into a c-shape as if holding a cup in your hand. Take your hand up to your mouth as if drinking from the cup.

Milk: Use both hands, make them into a fist, open hand and repeat. Looks like you are milking a cow.

Juice: Make a "J". Point your pinkie at your mouth with your palm facing forward. Then rotate your hand so palm is facing you.

More

More: Place your fingers and thumb together to make an O shape. Bring your hands together, tapping finger tips. Repeat a few times.

Book

Book: Put your hands together, palm to palm. Then holding your pinkies together, open up your hands as if opening a book.

Tired

Tired: Extend your fingers and hold them together. Start with your fingers touching your chest and roll your hands forward. Use facial expression to show you are tired.

Bed

Bed: Bring both hands together, place them at the side of your slightly tilted head. Rest your head on your hands. Looks like resting your head on a pillow.

Sleep

Sleep: Start with your hands over your eyes, fingers spread apart. Move your hand down your face to your chin. Bring fingers together at chin. Close your eyes.

I Love You

I Love You: Point index finger to chest. Cross your arms. Point index finger to person.

I Love You

I Love You is a combination of an "I", "L" and "Y". Shake hand back and forth.

Finished

Finished: Hold both open hands to the front with palms facing self and fingers pointing up. Shake them quickly outward to the sides a few times.

Thank you for buying our book. We appreciate it. We hope you have fun signing! Come back and meet more of our friends.
                    Maribeth and Joanne

Tips for Teaching Your Baby Sign Language

Have Fun
As with any new skill, it's important to go at your baby's pace and keep it fun. The best time to start is when your baby begins to desire to communicate. This is usually around 9 or 10 months - you'll notice your baby is more sociable, starts to babble, and uses noises and facial expressions to get your attention.

Interests
Start with a sign he or she is interested in. Lots of babies quickly pick up the sign for "more" in relation to food!

Speak and Sign
Every time you use the word, show your baby the sign, too.

Repetition
Always use the same sign, use lots of repetition, and emphasize the key word along with the sign, so your baby can clearly see and hear the connection: "Do you want "milk"? "Here is your "milk".

Be Patient
Your baby may try the sign himself after a few days, or it may take several weeks - be patient. Make it as fun as you can. Babies are much more likely to learn from something they enjoy doing.

Encourage
Encourage and praise your child when he/she signs to you.

To see more of Joanne's artwork and murals visit
www.onceuponapaintedwall.com

Copyright © 2016 by Maribeth MacDonald
Illustrations copyright © 2016 by Joanne Coughlin

All rights reserved. Published in the United States by
Sparhawk Press, Boston, MA

For more information about the author visit:
www.signingwithmaribeth.com

For more information about the illustrator visit:
www.onceuponapaintedwall.com

CPSIA information can be obtained at www.ICGtesting.com
Printed in the USA
BVIW12n1640061016
464155BV00008B/16